Othes

The Nation's Memory

A pictorial guide to the
Public Record Office

Frontispiece: The Public Record Office
building in Chancery Lane viewed from
the west.

The Nation's Memory

A pictorial guide to the Public Record Office

Edited by Jane Cox

with contributions by David Thomas, Timothy Padfield and Michael Jubb

London: Her Majesty's Stationery Office

"Up, and by water . . . to the Temple; and thence to the Chapel of Rolles, where I made enquiry for several Rolles and was soon informed in the manner of it, . . . I hired a clerk there to read to me about twelve or more several rolls which I did call for; and it was a great pleasure to me to see the method in which the the Rolles are kept"

Diary of Samuel Pepys 15 March 1669

". . . The most remarkable fact which emerges from the story is that for once the Stat^y Office is in a position to make a better bargain than a private Co; and I feel abased before them when I reflect on the many uncomplimentary remarks which I have passed on their methods at different times."

Extract of letter from Sir Geo Murray, Secretary GPO to Gleadowe HMT, dated 19 April 1902, on printing of the Telephone Directory (Paper 11770 in T1/9864A/16064)

Contents

Photographs by

John Millen   4, 13, 15, 21, 22, 33, 34, 35, 36, 37, 38, 39, 40, 41, 42, 43, 44, 45, 46, 47, 49, 50, 51, 52, 54, 56, 57, 60, 61, 62, 64, 65, 66, 67, 68, 69, 70, 72, 74

Christopher Cormack   8, 16, 18, 19, 26, 27, 63, 75, 76

Mo Wilson   2, 6, 14, 20, 23, 31, 32

The National Maritime Museum   48, 77, 78

The National Portrait Gallery   55a, 55b, 58

The Property Services Agency   frontispiece, 3, 28

The Greater London Record Office Picture Library   71, 73

PRO Collection   1, 30

PRO Slide Collection   11, 12

Steven Morris   9, 29

The Builder magazine   5, 7, 25

Cecil Beaton, Camera Press, London   59

David Reed   24

The Imperial War Museum   53

The Mary Evans Picture Library   10

The Morning Star   17

Design by HMSO Graphic Design

Introduction

The records of British Government and Law have been said to 'excel all others in age beauty, correctness and authority.' Documenting the history of a medieval kingdom, a world-wide empire and an emerging welfare state, they run in virtually unbroken series from the eleventh century to the present era. For scholars, lawyers, genealogists and journalists there is a wealth of information to be found, and for anyone interested in this county's heritage there are untold treasures.

Most of the archive is kept in the Public Record Office, which was founded in 1838 and put in charge of a senior judge, the master of the rolls until it was transferred to the lord chancellor's care in 1959.

The two main buildings, the original repository in London, in Chancery Lane and the new one at Kew house the ninety shelf-miles of material which has accumulated to date. Nineteenth century census returns may be read on microfilm in the Land Registry building in Portugal Street.

This guide explains the services offered by the Public Record Office and attempts to convey something of the range, value and fascination of the records.

1   The Rolls House and Chapel, which were demolished in 1892 to make room for an extension to the Public Record Office.

2   The main search room, the Round Room.

The Buildings

The Chancery Lane Building

The Public Record Office's original building is a major monument of Victorian London. The fine gothic structure straddles the boundary between the cities of London and Westminster, lying between Chancery Lane and Fetter Lane in the heart of legal London. It was built in several phases over a period of fifty one years, between 1851 and 1902, on a site which had been associated with the storage of government records since the middle ages, the Rolls Estate.

The history of the site can be traced back to the thirteenth century when it was occupied by a house for converted Jews. When the Jews were expelled from the country, the property was handed over to the master of the rolls, who was, in times past, not a judge, but, as his title suggests, the keeper of the parchment rolls which were the records of the king's Chancery. When, in 1836, a Select Committee recommended the building of a single repository to store the records of government, the eighteenth-century Rolls House was no longer the residence of the master of the rolls; he had moved to a more fashionable part of London and it was being used, as a store for some of the Chancery records. After a great deal of debate as to whether the records ought to be kept in Westminster near the centre of government, the estate was vested in the Crown as a site for the new record office.

Sir James Pennethorne, the surveyor of buildings to the Office of Woods and Works, and a pupil of Nash, designed the first two blocks, which lie at the centre and east of the present building. The foundation stone was laid in May 1851 and in 1868 work was completed on the eastern block, which contains three public search rooms, the most impressive of which is a circular room rising through the full height of the building and top-lit by a glass roof. Pennethorne's record office was built solidly of iron and stone, to withstand fire and accommodate the heavy loads of records. The facing is of Kentish rag, decorated with the coats of arms and mottoes of officers of state. Twenty-four years later a further wing was added, facing onto Chancery Lane, and the

3   Turrets on Pennethorne's Building.

4 Queues at Chancery Lane in the early 1960s.

Rolls Chapel was pulled down and a museum for the exhibiting of records erected on its site. Sir John Taylor was the architect for this part of the building, which was of Babbacombe limestone and contained a handsome set of offices for the staff.

With the proliferation of government departments and activities more and more paper was created and greater space was needed for the storage of records. And more people wanted to look at them. The small search rooms designed by Pennethorne for a handful of historians and antiquarians were hopelessly inadequate for the floods of students brought in by the expansion of budgets for postgraduate research in the early 1960s. The queues down Chancery Lane were lengthened by the increasing hordes of family historians, eager to chronicle the doings of their ancestors from the public records. Agitation for more space, which had begun in 1934, culminated in the opening of a new building in Kew in 1977.

The Kew Building

Ten years after it was opened, Kew still attracts archivists and architects from all over the world who want to know about the design of modern archive buildings.

A primary design requirement of the building was to speed the production of records to the public, and so a square shape was chosen to minimise the distance documents have to be moved. At the centre of the square is a distribution core with lifts, a stairway and most important, an automatic vertical document conveyor or paternoster. This transports the documents from the storage areas to a distribution area giving onto the reading rooms. There staff sort records on arrival into banks of pigeon holes labelled by reading room seat numbers, one pigeon hole to each seat.

The storage areas occupy the top three floors. Each one has an area of about 7,400m². They are equipped with about 110,000 metres of steel shelving. Records too large to be moved in the paternoster are stored on the second floor with maps and plans and produced in a special reading room on that floor.

5   The Kew building at night.

The other aim in designing Kew was to provide the maximum protection for its contents against their main enemies: heat, damp, insects, light, pollution and fire. The atmosphere is controlled by a complex air-conditioning system which maintains a stable temperature and relative humidity, as well as filtering out pollutant dusts and some gases. Lighting is also carefully controlled. The storage areas are lit by double coated tubular fluorescent lamps. The small slit windows are designed to minimise the amount of ultra-violet light falling on the documents while avoiding the impression of a completely enclosed working environment.

Each of the storage floors is divided into three fire-proof compartments; the doors between them being held open on fusible links so that they will close automatically in the event of fire. Smoke detectors, dry risers and fixed hose reels, together with a smoke venting system complete the protection against fire and in each corner of the building there is a protected fire escape.

The public areas of the building consist of a reception hall, a restaurant and cloakrooms on the ground floor, whilst the first floor contains the Reference Room accommodating lists, registers, indexes and other means of reference to the records. This is staffed by search department officers who are available to assist any of the public needing help. Adjoining the Reference Room is the Langdale Room, the main reading room. 248 readers can be seated at the specially designed octagonal tables, giving each reader a clearly defined work

6   The Reference Room.

4

area equipped with a pull-out bookrest and an electrical supply. The room is comfortable and quiet and is illuminated by overhead lighting and by very large windows. The upper floors are cantilevered over the reading rooms to prevent sunlight shining directly onto the windows. Photocopies and micro-film can be ordered at a counter directly accessible to the readers. On the other side of the reference room is another reading room, the Romilly Room, housing a microfilm reading room.

The rest of the first floor and most of the ground floor are occupied by staff offices and conservation and reprographic workshops.

The building is a reinforced concrete framed structure resting on a raft foundation. The floors are supported on a grid of columns, the lift-shafts and stair-wells are enclosed within reinforced concrete walls, and the building is faced with brown pre-cast concrete slabs.

In 1977 Kew was a radical departure; not only was the building itself new but so were many of the systems within it: the computer generated *Current Guide,* the automated ordering system, the bleepers used to inform readers their documents were available, even the standard format of the lists of records. By the late 1990s Kew will be full and new accommodation is already being planned. New developments in information technology and architectural design will be utilised to make the building of the 1990s as radical a concept as was the building of the 1970s.

8 Some items from the public records, including:

a An agreement between the Earl of Chester and Lincoln and the men of Frieston and Butterwick, Lincolnshire. (DL 27/270)

b Quill (SR 67/12/9)

c The Red Book of the Exchequer (E 164/2)

d Font from the Rolls Chapel

e The death mask of Dr. Yonge, a master of the rolls

f The Domesday Chest

g Exchequer tallies (E 402/30)

h The pension book of Lord Montgomery of Alamein (PIN 900/43)

i Probate inventories (PROB 4)

j Gold Seal of Francis I in a bag (E 30/1109)

k Deed box (SR 67/12)

l Great Cowcher of Furness Abbey (DL 42/3)

m An optical disc

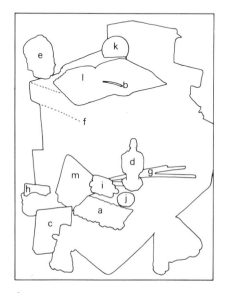

From parchment rolls to optical discs

A public record is any physical relic which conveys information about government transaction, whether it is a notched stick recording a debt of a few shillings to the medieval Exchequer, a scribbled note by a Tudor king or a formal Cabinet minute. The Public Record Office holds the records of the central law courts as well as those of the business of direct ruling; in earlier times the functions were inextricably linked. Legal records relate to disputes between subjects as well as to criminal prosecutions, and some of the more bizarre items exhibited in court have found their way into the state archive: plaster casts, nail clippings, pieces of hair and the like. Most public records are written on parchment or paper in manuscript or, equally in recent years, typescript, but increasingly electrostatic copies are to be found and electronic records on tapes and discs are also being transferred for preservation.

Although the Office does not set out to collect private papers, it holds the papers of four prime ministers, Chatham, Pitt, Russell and MacDonald; in addition, letters, diaries and other things of a personal nature have found their way into the official records. A clerk or minister may have left private letters in a desk drawer which were bundled up and packed away with his official correspondence.

The records span 900 years, the earliest being that phenomenal survey of the kingdom conducted by William the Conqueror which the Anglo-Saxons nicknamed 'Domesday'. With no revolutionaries or invaders to destroy them the queen's records have remained virtually intact from the early middle ages. Until the mid-nineteenth century they were kept, by and large, in the office or courts which created them. When the cupboards and shelves started to overflow they might be sent off to be stored somewhere else. Access was restricted in a rather haphazard way; there were as many record keepers as there were repositories, and each guarded his charges jealously. Only the tenacious and the relentlessly inquisitive could get to see them and use them for historical or legal purposes. With the nineteenth century came stirrings of

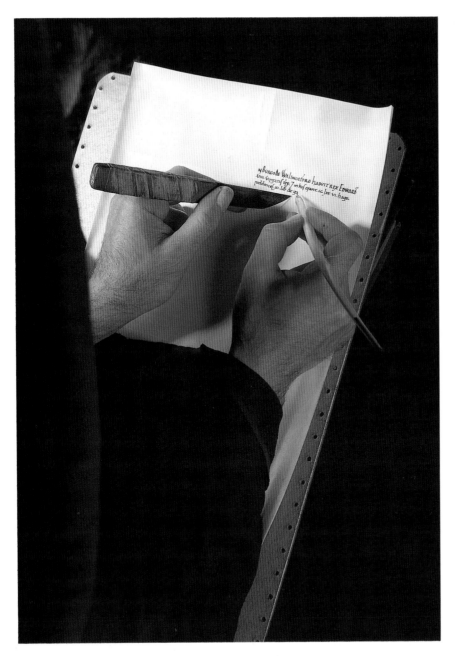

9   In the middle ages, writing was done with a sharpened feather on parchment or vellum (sheep, goat, calf or deer skin). The picture shows a monk 'writing Domesday': he has a scratching tool in his left hand for correcting mistakes.

10   Typewriters were used by the Civil Service from the 1870s.

a scientific approach to history and a new consciousness of the importance of original sources. Between 1800 and 1837 six Royal Commissions agonised over the problem of the state's archives. In 1838 the Public Record Office was established by Act of Parliament, to take care and control of the legal records, which included medieval administrative records of the Chancery and Exchequer and fourteen years later all departmental records were brought under its auspices. From 60 different storehouses the sacks and parcels of rolls and writs and files were brought into Pennethorne's repository in Chancery Lane; from the Tower, the Chapter House in Westminster Abbey, the State Paper Office in Carlton Ride and all the nooks and crannies where they had been hidden.

As soon as there was somewhere official for them to be stored the records kept appearing, as it were, from nowhere. By 1928 there were 35 miles of shelves' full. Government now produces in one year enough paperwork to fill 100 miles of shelves. A carefully devised system of inspection has evolved which ensures that a proper selection is made whereby all that is necessary for practical purposes is retained and enough of the rest to document the history of the nation and its people. In 1954 the report of the Grigg Committee laid down the principles: files were to be reviewed after five years in the departments and the reviewers were to ask themselves if the records were of any continuing use. The committee reckoned that anything of lasting historical value would survive that process. When the files were 25 years old, or the oldest paper on them was of that age, then they would be looked at again by the department and the Public Record Office together. The records

11   Newly arrived records in the intermediate repository at Hayes.

12 Selecting records for permanent preservation.

selected after the second review should be transferred to the Office unless the department still needed them for administrative use. About a shelf mile of records are taken in every year.

With the advent of the quantitative approach to history, the counting of cases and the compilation of statistics, there has been a need for vast masses of evidence and an increasing demand for long runs of records to be preserved which might have no intrinsic value in themselves. The growth of interest in family history has exacerbated the problem. For neither group of researchers was the old system of keeping papers which related to famous cases or events of any use. It is no comfort to the genealogist who wants every scrap of information about his ancestors preserved to know that if he were the son of Lord Montgomery of Alamein his father's pension book would be one of the very few kept in the state archives. It is no good to the historian of the distribution of wealth in the early nineteenth century if the death duty accounts of Jane Austen and a few other luminaries are kept and the rest thrown away. To accommodate the social, administrative and economic historian, a system of sampling was introduced and a careful watch is kept for particularly fruitful sources for the genealogist.

13   A photograph of Ramsay
MacDonald, the first Labour Prime
Minister, from his papers in the PRO.
(PRO 30/69)

14 The actor Donald Sinden in the
Long Room at Chancery Lane.

15 The surrender document of
Robertsbridge Abbey bearing the
signature of Mr Sinden's ancestor,
William Senden. (E 322/203)

Research

Access

It comes as a surprise to many that anyone who is able to produce some sort of formal identification like a bank card or a driving licence, can be issued with a reader's ticket and come into the Public Record Office and search for himself among the records of the state. Any members of the public may order up a Chancery roll from the reign of King John, open it up and read it, if he can make sense of the abbreviated Latin. He can pore over tax lists from the time of the Black Death or relive his experiences in World War Two by reading his unit's War Diary. Historians, genealogists, journalists, lawyers and the simply curious come to find material for books, articles and pedigrees and to answer questions about the past.

Provided that the records are at least 30 years old, and have survived, they are, in most cases, open to all. Only if there is something contained in a file or register which is deemed to continue to be personally or publicly sensitive is the closure period extended. Records of courts martial, for instance, are closed for 75 years and out of respect for the pledge of confidentiality which was made when the information was collected, census returns are closed for 100 years. At the beginning of January each year a new batch of records is made available to the public.

Some of the more heavily used records may be read only on microfilm; had the original 1851 census enumerators' books continued to be subject to handling by eager family and local historians, there would now be little of them left.

16   Assize records closed until 1997.

How to start

In the Public Record Office's ninety miles of shelves full of bulging files, leathery registers, notebooks, sacks and rolls there are millions of facts and names. Because of the huge quantity of material the reader's chief problem

17   The annual release of thirty year old records.

is finding a starting point. There is no general index of names, places or subjects, and for most new readers, familiar with the author and subject catalogues in libraries, the system is rather bewildering. The records are arranged and classified according to their provenance and given a letter code roughly corresponding to the department or court whence they came; thus WO for War Office and other departments concerned with the administration of the Army, ED for departments concerned with education, AN for post-nationalisation railway records, etc. The records are described in the *Current Guide* which runs into many volumes (it is also available on microfiche). Part one is an alpha-numerical list of all the records, starting with A (Alienation Office) and going through to ZPER (periodicals from the British Transport Historical Records). Part two is an administrative history of the departments and courts, and Part three is an index to the other two. Many new readers find that the series of Information sheets (listed on p. 54) are helpful when starting a search, and there are some useful handbooks (listed on p. 56).

The Information Sheet, handbook or *Current Guide* will refer the reader to a list of records. Each letter code, such as WO or ED contains a series of numbered classes such as WO 97, Soldiers' Discharge Documents, and for each class there is a list, which is usually arranged chronologically (See illustration 19). The list is the key means of reference and can be consulted on the search room shelves at Chancery Lane and in the Reference Room at Kew. From it the reader takes the reference number for the item he wishes to consult, keys that reference into a computer terminal – waits for a short time for the document to be delivered to the service counter. At Kew there is a 'bleeper' system to announce the arrival of the document; at Chancery Lane a check has to be made at the counter.

For some classes of records the list is a sparse inventory, supplying little information, but there may be additional finding aids in the form of the indexes which were the working tools of the clerks in the department or court when the records were in daily use. Those may be name, place or subject indexes which will save the searcher an immense amount of time, even though the arrangements may seem bizarre to the modern eye. The wills of some princesses proved in the Prerogative Court of Canterbury, for instance, are indexed under 'S' for 'serenissima' (highness). Illustration 18 shows a seventeenth-century Chancery index to decrees (C 33/115).

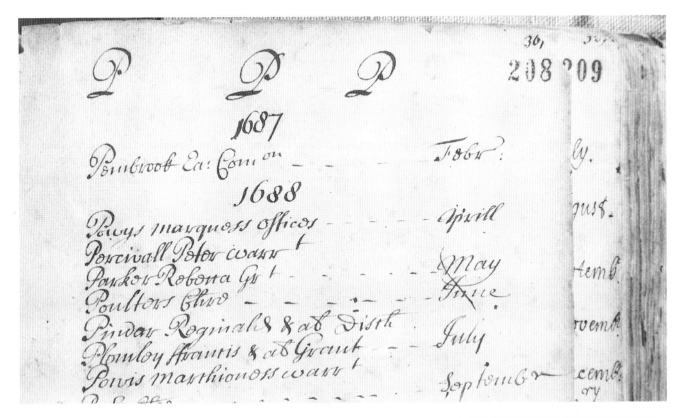

18 A seventeenth century index to Chancery Decrees. (C 33/115)

Reference	PARISH FILES		ED 2
ED 2	Date	File No.	Description
			BEDFORDSHIRE
1	1871–1891	1	Ampthill
	1871–1898	2	Arlesey
	1871–1886	3	Aspley Guise
	1885–1898	3A	Aspley Heath
	1871–1872	3B	Astwick
	1871–1895	5	Battlesden and Potsgrove
	1871–1873	7	Biggleswade
	1871–1884	11	Bolnhurst

19 A modern list of records. (ED 2)

20   Reading records on microfilm in
the Rolls Room at Chancery Lane.

The search rooms are open from 9.30 to 5pm Monday to Friday. Last orders for documents are taken at 3.30pm. Orders for documents may be made by phone if the full reference is given. A wide range of reprographic services is offered including infra-red photography for faded manuscripts. Only pencils or typewriters may be used for taking notes. There are three sites where records may be read:

Chancery Lane:
Medieval and early modern records, all legal records, 1841 and 1851 census returns, wills, non-conformist registers.

Portugal Street:
1841, 1851, 1861, 1871, 1881 census returns

Kew:
Modern departmental records, including records of military and naval service.

A detailed list of the division of record groups between Chancery Lane and Kew is given on p. 28.

Preservation

Archives, unlike printed books, are unique. Each parchment membrane or paper page among the public records contains text which is not normally reproduced elsewhere, and immense care has to be taken to make sure that the document does not perish and the information become lost.

When Pennethorne designed the repository in Chancery Lane, he provided for very thick walls which would maintain the stable environmental conditions suitable for keeping parchment and paper. By the time the Kew building was under construction there were British standards for the storage of archives to provide more precise guidance. But in the years before there was any purpose-built accommodation, a large proportion of the records was stored in most undesirable conditions, subject to damp, rats and neglect.

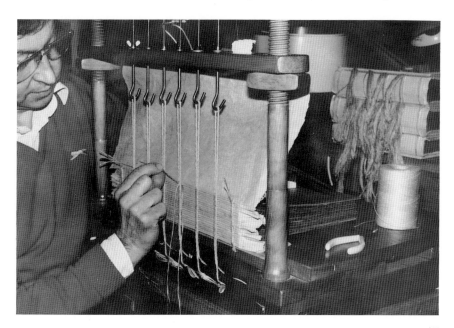

21   Rebinding Domesday in 1985.

Even some of the documents which were made after the Office came into being have not avoided decay. There is an alarming large quantity of flimsy acid papers which contain the source of their own decay. Other documents have been stored in unsuitable conditions before transfer to the Office; many have been damaged by excessive or careless handling by their originators or subsequent users.

The Office has a Conservation Department which exists to save documents from destruction by any source of decay. The staff of trained conservators are skilled in all necessary techniques to repair documents so that they can be used while maintaining them in the form in which they were first created. This process does not attempt to conceal repairs: it is a principle of archive conservation that restoration of the lost original text should not be attempted.

Parchment and early paper documents are all repaired by hand, using modern toned parchment and paper to fill in missing portions of the document. More modern paper items are normally repaired using a much faster but less satisfactory technique of lamination, which involves bonding a strong tissue to either side of each page under pressure in a hot press. Some maps are dry mounted using similar methods, while others are repaired by hand and mounted on paper or linen. All sorts of books, from the eleventh century to the twentieth, are rebound or rebacked by hand in the bindery.

23 A conservator at Kew repairing eighteenth century East Florida Claims Commission Papers.

Detailed attention is paid as well to other materials: photographs, textiles, seals and metal buttons are all repaired with special techniques.

There are many fragile items, including reams of poor quality modern paper, which are impossible to conserve with traditional processes like lamination because of their bulk. They would probably be best left alone but there is little purpose in keeping records at all if they are not to be read. The deterioration of the most popular classes has been halted by an extensive filming programme (the film library now contains well over a thousand miles of microfilm) and by making fragile or heavily used records available for consultation only in the form of microfilm.

24   A strong room in Chancery Lane,
showing parchment rolls laid on the
slate shelving.

25   The repository area at Kew.

26   Microfilming records at Chancery Lane.

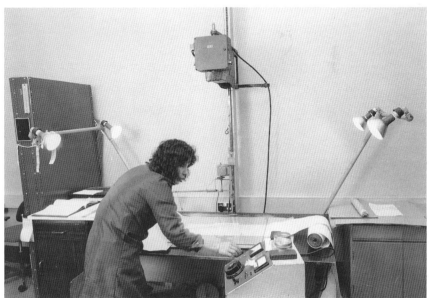

27 The Public Record Office's museum in Chancery Lane was designed to retain the style of the Rolls Chapel. Three monuments which had been in the chapel were re-erected, those of (from left to right): Richard Allington of Lincoln's Inn, d.1561 (the Master of the Rolls was his executor); Edward, Lord Bruce of Kinloss, Master of the Rolls, d.1611; and Dr John Yonge, Master of the Rolls, d.1516. The latter is the work of the celebrated Pietro Torrigiano.

28 Domesday in the case designed for the 1986 exhibition.

Exhibitions

29   Souvenirs sold at the Domesday exhibition.

It was nearly fifty years after the founding of the PRO in 1838 before records were first displayed to the public as well as being made available in the search rooms. The eight-hundredth anniversary of Domesday Book was commemorated in 1886 by a small exhibition held in the Round Room. That exhibition was restricted to a small and largely scholarly audience. But sixteen years later, the extension of the Chancery Land building offered the opportunity to mount a permanent display. For the first time, ordinary members of the public were able to see a selection of notable documents among the public records, without having to acquire a reader's ticket to study them in the search rooms.

When the old Rolls Chapel was demolished, it was decided to erect a new museum on the site to show a selection of records alongside some of the monuments from the chapel. The new museum, which opened in 1902, displayed some 250 documents, ranging in date from Domesday Book to Queen Victoria's Coronation Roll. The exhibition was arranged partly so as to illustrate the principal archival groups of records, from Chancery, the Exchequer, and the major government departments; and partly to bring together letters and other papers by and about famous people and events. There were thus displays of medieval charters and accounts, despatches from military commanders from Drake to Nelson and Wellington, letters of literary figures such as Jonson, Spenser and Addison, and royal letters and signatures. Later more documents were added to the display, some in drawers underneath the showcases. The general scheme of the display remained unaltered, however, and even when new cases were installed and the display was re-arranged in 1955, most of the 350 exhibits were the same as those selected in 1902.

In order to restrict the records' exposure to light, the museum was open to the public only on weekday afternoons, although groups of schoolchildren and others could arrange to visit at other times.

30   Her Majesty The Queen in the parchment making room at the Domesday exhibition, 29 May 1986.

31   The Age of Chivalry exhibition at the Royal Academy, spring 1988. The Public Record Office lent, amongst other things, an account roll itemising expenditure on the building of Charing Cross, one of the twelve crosses erected by Edward I in memory of his wife, Eleanor of Castile. (E 101/353/1).

32   The statue of Queen Eleanor, taken from the cross at Waltham. (Victoria and Albert Museum)

Since the 1920s, small displays had been mounted for special groups visiting the Office, and between 1948 and 1963 a series of exhibitions was held in a room near the museum. There were exhibitions to illustrate the Office's holdings of records such as treaties, and to celebrate special occasions such as the 350th anniversary of the founding of the state of Virginia in 1957, or the Queen's tour of the Commonwealth in 1954. There was a break of more than twenty years between the last such exhibition and the mounting of the Domesday Exhibition, to celebrate the 900th anniversary of Domesday Book, in 1986. For the first time all the documents associated with Domesday and its compilation were brought together, along with computers and audio-visual displays. Over 130,000 people came to see the oldest and most famous public record of all.

A new display of records was opened in 1988 in a room adjacent to the former museum. It is arranged in themes, from the law through the records of warfare to the welfare state. In order to preserve the documents, the displays are changed at appropriate intervals, though the thematic arrangement stays the same. Temporary exhibitions are being arranged in the old museum on the site of the Rolls Chapel, starting with an exhibition in 1989 of railway records. In this way the contents of the PRO are being made known to the increasing numbers of people who are interested to see its treasures.

Since 1958, the Office has also been able to lend records for exhibition elsewhere. Loans have been made to national institutions such as the Victoria and Albert Museum and the National Portrait Gallery and also to local museums and galleries in Leeds, Gloucester and elsewhere. The exhibitions have ranged in scale from a display in a single showcase at the British Library to celebrate George Borrow's centenary in 1980, to the Age of Chivalry exhibition at the Royal Academy in 1988, and the records from twelfth-century writs through charters and military maps, to posters and patent specifications. The Office also makes increasing numbers of loans to overseas countries.

The Records

Some idea of the span and scope of the Public Record Office's holdings can be had from a glance at the list of the division of records between the two main buildings (see p. 28). It would be impossible in a guide of this length to attempt more than to give a taste of what is on offer. The records of what is now the Foreign and Commonwealth Office alone run into more than 2000 classes, of which one alone, General Correspondence after 1906, Political (FO 371), occupies 9,369 feet of shelves and comprises 125, 456 volumes and files.

As the functions of government grew, changed and extended, so the volume of records swelled. The early medieval kings had a handful of literate clerics who travelled round the country with the court and wrote down anything that was important on treated animal skins. It was like running a private estate; taxes had to be collected and land grants made; there were small territorial squabbles with neighbouring counties. Gradually things changed and the government interfered in matters that had been left to the church or private individuals. Public authorities began to run medical services as once the monks had done and provide pensions instead of relying on the alms of the pious. Industry, farming and education became public concerns; there were more rules, more instructions, more forms. The population grew and Britain involved herself decisively with the rest of the world.

33   Thirteenth century Patent and Charter rolls.

Division of Record Groups between Chancery Lane and Kew

Records at Chancery Lane*

Admiralty, High Court of (HCA)
Alienation Office (A)
Assize, Clerks of (ASSI)
Bankruptcy, Court of (B)
Central Criminal Court (CRIM)
Chancery (C)
Chester, Palatinate of (CHES)
Common Pleas, Court of (CP)
County Courts (AK)
Crown Estate Commissioners (CRES)
Delegates, Court of (DEL)
Durham, Palatinate of (DURH)
Exechequer (E)
    Auditors of Land Revenue (LR)
General Register Office (RG)
    Census Returns (RG 9-RG 10),
    Non-Parochial Registers and records
    (RG 4-RG 8) and certain other
    registers and associated papers
    (RG 18, 19, 27, 30-37, 43) only
Home Office (HO 107)
    Census Returns 1841 and 1851 only
Inland Revenue, Board of (IR 26)
    Estate Duty Registers only (IR27)
Judicature, Supreme Court of (J)
Justices Itinerant (JUST)
King's Bench, Court of (KB)
King's Bench Prison (PRIS)
Lancaster, Duchy of (DL)
Lancaster, Palatinate of (PL)
Land Revenue Record Office (LRRO)
Law Officers' Department (LO)
Lord Chamberlain's Department (LC)
Lord Steward's Department (LS)
Palace Court (PALA)
Peveril, Court of the Honour of (PEV)

Prerogative Court of
    Canterbury (PROB)
Privy Council, Judicial Committee of
    the (PCAP)
Privy Council Office (PC)
Privy Purse Office (PP)
Privy Seal Office (PSO)
Public Prosecutions, Director of (DPP)
Public Record Office (PRO)
    Transcripts (PRO 31) and certain
    classes of gifts and deposits
    (PRO 30)**
Queen Anne's Bounty (QAB)
Requests, Court of (REQ)
Signet Office (SO)
Special Collections (SC)
Star Chamber, Court of (STAC)
State Paper Office (SP)
Treasury Solicitor (TS)
Wales, Principality of (WALE)
Wards & Liveries, Court of (WARD)

Records at Kew

Admiralty (ADM)
Advisory, Conciliation & Arbitration
    Service (CW)
Agriculture, Fisheries & Food, Ministry
    of (MAF)
Air Ministry (AIR)
Aviation, Ministry of (AVIA)
British Council (BW)
British Railways Board (AN)
British Transport Docks Board (BR)
British Transport Historical Records
    (RAIL) (ZLIB) (ZPER) (ZSPC)
Cabinet Office (CAB)

Captured Enemy Documents (GFM)
Central Midwives Board (DV)
Certification Office for Trade Unions
    and Employers' Associations (CL)
Civil Aviation Authority (DR)
Civil Service Commission (CSC)
Civil Service Department (BA)
Civil Service Pay Research
    Unit (CSPR)
Coal Industry Social Welfare
    Organisation (BX)
Colonial Office (CO)
Consumer Council (AJ)
Copyright Office (COPY)
Countryside Commission (COU)
Crown Agents for Overseas
    Governments and
    Administrations (CAOG)
Customs & Excise, Board of (CUST)
Defence, Ministry of (DEFE)
Defunct Temporary Bodies (BS)
Development Commission (D)
Dominions Office and Commonwealth
    Relations Office (DO)
Education & Science, Department
    of (ED)
Educational Technology, Council
    for (EA)
Energy, Department of (EG)
Environment, Department of the (AT)
Environmental Pollution, Royal
    Commission on (CY)
Exchequer and Audit
    Department (AO)
Export Credits Guarantee
    Department (ECG)
Foreign and Commonwealth
    Office (FCO)
Foreign Office (FO)
Forestry Commission (F)
Forfeited Estates, Commissioners
    of (FEC)
Friendly Societies, Registry of (FS)
General Nursing Council (DT)
General Register Office (RG)
    except Census Returns (RG 9-RG
    10), Non-Parochial Registers and

records (RG 4-RG 8) and certain other registers and associated papers (RG 18, 19, 27, 30-37, 43)

Government Actuary's Department (ACT)

Health and Safety Commission and Executive (EF)

Health & Social Security, Department of (BN)

Health, Ministry of (MH)

Health Visitors, Council for the Education and Training of (DW)

Historical Manuscripts Commission (HMC)

Home Office (HO) except Census Returns (HO 107)

Housing & Local Government, Ministry of (HLG)

Hudson's Bay Company (BH) Microfilm. Access by permission of the Company only

Information, Central Office of (INF)

Inland Revenue, Board of (IR) except Estate Duty Registers (IR 26 and IR 27)

International Organisations (DG) records of International Whaling Commission and Western European Union

Irish Sailors' & Soldiers' Land Trust (AP)

Iron and Steel Board (BE)

Joint Board of Clinical Nursing Studies (DY)

Labour, Ministry of (LAB)

Land Registry (LAR)

Lands Tribunal (LT)

Law Commission (BC)

Local Government Boundary Commission for England (AX)

Local Government Boundary Commission for Wales (DD)

Location of Offices Bureau (AH)

London Gazette (ZJ)

Lord Chancellor's Office (LCO)

Manpower Services Commission (ET)

Meteorological Office (BJ)

Metropolitan Police Office (MEPO)

Monuments, Ancient & Historic in Wales and Monmouthshire, Royal Commission on (MONW)

Monuments, Historic (England), Royal Commission on (AE)

Munitions, Ministry of (MUN)

National Academic Awards, Council for (DB)

National Assistance Board (AST)

National Coal Board (COAL)

National Debt Office (NDO)

National Dock Labour Board (BK)

National Incomes Commission (NICO)

National Insurance Audit Department (NIA)

National Playing Fields Association (CB)

National Ports Council (DK)

National Savings, Department for (NSC)

National Service, Ministry of (NATS)

Northern Ireland Office (CJ)

Occupational Pensions Board (DM)

Ordnance Survey Department (OS)

Overseas Development, Ministry of, and Overseas Development Administration (OD)

Parliamentary Boundary Commission (AF)

Parliamentary Papers (ZHC) (ZHL)

Parole Board (BV)

Paymaster General's Office (PMG)

Pensions & National Insurance, Ministry of (PIN)

Pensions Appeal Tribunal (BF)

Post Office Users' National Council (DJ)

Power, Ministry of (POWE)

Price Commission (CX)

Prime Minister's Office (PREM)

Prison Commission (PCOM)

Public Building & Works, Ministry of (WORK)

Public Health Laboratory Services Board (DN)

Public Record Office (PRO) all classes except transcripts (PRO 31) and certain classes of gifts and deposits (PRO 30)**

Public Trustee Office (PT)

Public Works Loan Board (PWLB)

Racial Equality, Commission for (CK)

Reconstruction, Ministry of (RECO)

Remploy Ltd (BM)

Research Institutes (AY)

Royal Fine Arts Commission (BP)

Royal Mint (MINT)

Scientific & Industrial Research, Department of (DSIR)

Sessional Papers, House of Commons (ZHC) House of Lords (ZHL)

Social Security Commissioners (CT)

Stationery Office (STAT)

Supply, Ministry of (SUPP)

Tithe Redemption Commission (TITH)

Trade, Board of (BT)

Transport, Ministry of (MT)

Treasury (T)

Tribunals, Council on (BL)

United Kingdom Atomic Energy Authority (AB)

University Grants Committee (UGC)

Value Added Tax Tribunals (CV)

Wallace Collection (AR)

War Office (WO)

Welsh Office (BD)

*   Some classes to be seen at Chancery Lane are housed at Hayes, Middlesex, and notice of several working days is required.

** PRO 30/5, 18-19, 21, 23-26, 28, 34, 38, 41, 44, 47, 49, 50, 53 and 80 are at Chancery Lane.
    PRO 31/20 is at Kew.
    PRO 30/4, 13-15, 62 are no longer held in the Public Record Office

The central operation of government.

The kingdom of England was an entity long before the Norman invasion and its written records predate what we refer to as the public records. About a thousand charters of early kings survive in The British Library, college libraries and elsewhere, the recipients' copies of formal letters granting land or privileges. In the tenth century kings had started a revolution by using what may seem to the modern observer an obvious device, the writ, a very short, simple letter of instruction to royal officers or subjects, written in the vernacular.

By the time of the Conquest, it seems, there was a fairly sophisticated Chancery or government secretariat, but, the official records do not start until the reign of King John. At this time the clerks of the Chancery started

34 The king's orders issued in small sealed letters.

35 The Great Seal of Henry I.
(DL 10/23)

the practice of copying the 'out-letters' on to parchment membranes, two feet in length and a foot wide. The skins were sewn end to end until they were 30 or 40 feet long and then rolled up. These are the famous rolls of Chancery which were perpetuated into the present century. They changed in content, of course; the early Patent Rolls, for instance, contain a great variety of material, letters about policy making and foreign negotiations, whilst the later rolls have only land grants, appointments of officers of state and the registration of inventions. There are over 26,000 rolls in the two main series, the Patent Rolls for open or formal letters, and the Close Rolls, for closed or informal correspondence and instructions. The 'in-letters' which survive from this early period were brought together from various sources and places and now comprise two artificial collections known as Ancient Correspondence and Ancient Petitions.

As the years passed Chancery became increasingly involved in the routine issue of formal documents and judicial matters. Under the Tudor monarchs the business of government was conducted in a less formal manner by the king and a small council and the important state correspondence and papers were kept by the king's private secretaries instead of the chancellor. This series of records, which comprises in-letters from home and abroad, entry books of out-letters, minutes of Privy Council and committee meetings, notes, memoranda and a host of miscellaneous items, came to be known as the State Papers. They are the chief source for political and administrative history for the sixteenth and seventeenth centuries.

Towards the end of the eighteenth century the business of government became too much for two secretaries and their staff to handle and the modern departments of state began to emerge, each with a secretary in charge. The inner core of the Privy Council became the Cabinet. The home secretary was responsible for domestic affairs and a huge volume of records document the business of his department.

Since the middle of the last century state involvement in many new domestic matters has meant a proliferation of departments and agencies, such as the Departments of Health and Social Security, of Employment, of the Environment, and of Education and Science and the Ministry of Agriculture, Fisheries and Food.

36 Letters Patent for the founding of
Morpeth Grammar School by Edward VI.
By the Tudor period the recipients of
royal grants were given elaborate,
illuminated documents. (FEC 1/W30)

37 A list of people prosecuted for not
going to church in Stratford on Avon in
1592, found among the State Papers.
Among others named are John
Shakespeare, William's father, William
Fluellen and George Bardolph.
(SP 12/243/76 f. 212v)

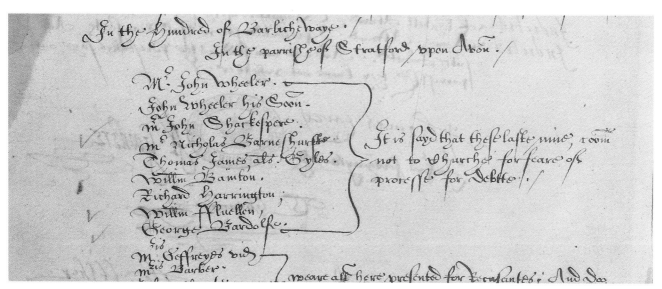

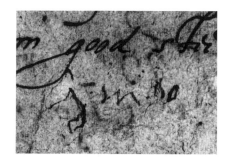

For six Minst Pyes of an Indifferent biggnesse:

[handwritten recipe]

38   A seventeenth century mince pie recipe found among the papers of one of James I's secretaries of state.
(SP 14/189/4)

For six Minst Pyes of an Indifferent biggnesse

Take halfe a peck of the fynest fflower, 2 lbs. of Suger, 2 lbs. of Butter, a Loyne of fatt Mutton, with a litle of a Legg of Veale to mynce with it. 2 lbs. of Reasons of the Sunn, as many Currons, of Cloves, Mace, and Nuttmeggs one ownce.
For the Paist mingle 1 pound a halfe of Suger with the fflower and breake in the Yolkes of six Eggs, then worke it together with 3 parts of the two pounde of Butter. Sett on a litle water and lett it Seethe, then scym it and put in the 4th parte of the Butter, and when it is melted, scym it cleane from the water and worke it with the Paist.
For the Meate let it be seasoned with Pepper, and mingled with halfe a pound of Sugar, the other ffrute and Spyce, the Raisons must be stoned, & some of them mynced amongst the meate, the others put in hole, put in the Joyce of two Orringes and one Leamond and the Ryne of them smale mynced.
When the Pyes are filled slyce dates and stick in the top and when you sett them into the oven wash them over with the yolkes of Eggs and pynn them upp in Papers.

39   Guy Fawkes's signature after torture. (SP 14/216/54)

40   An engraving showing the forcible dispersal of the reform meeting in St Peter's Fields, Manchester in 1819, known as Peterloo, from the main series of Home Office papers for this period.
(HO 42/199)

Government finance

From earliest times there was an official who was responsible for the king's treasure. The royal 'accounts department' which grew up in the twelfth century was called the Exchequer; it took its name from the chequer-board cloth on which the reckoning was done with counters. There was a system of enrolment, as in Chancery, but records were kept in duplicate and the rolls were made up in a different form; the top edges of the parchment membrane were fastened together rather than being sewn end to end. The most formal, impressive and best written series were the so-called Pipe Rolls, the earliest of which dates from 1129. Twice a year the sheriffs and other local officers of the crown were summoned to Westminster to answer their debts and the figures were noted on the rolls. From the time of Henry I to 1834 matters relating to crown finances may be found among the voluminous records of the Exchequer: such things as tax lists, pensions for royal servants, accounts for the building of palaces, and law suits. In the seventeenth century the Treasury evolved as the first of the modern departments of state and among its records there is a mass of correspondence relating to financial policy and other revenue matters.

41 Thirteenth-century tallies. Sticks were used by the Exchequer as receipts. The writing shows the names of people who had paid money into the Exchequer and the nature of the account; the notches indicate the sums to be paid.

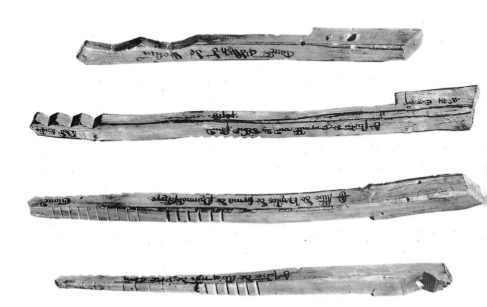

42 Early rolls.

43 An anti-semitic 'cartoon' on the
head of a thirteenth-century Jewish
receipt roll. (E 401/1565)

44   The foundation indenture of Henry VII's chapel. The most precious and valuable of the King's documents like Domesday, treaties and important deeds were kept in the King's treasury. (E 33/2)

Foreign affairs, war and the empire

The records of medieval diplomatic negotiations and wars are to be found among the Chancery and Exchequer archives described in the two previous sections, and there is a fine series of foreign State Papers for the seventeenth and eighteenth centuries. For the modern period there is a vast span of documentation from a number of sources: the Foreign Office, the War Office, the Admiralty, the Air Ministry, the Ministry of Defence. The later records do not concern themselves exclusively with the parleying of princes but take notice of Tommy in the trenches and nurses' pensions.

The colonising activities of the British brought a mass of correspondence into Westminster; the records of the Colonial Office and the Dominions Office provide detailed accounts of happenings in nearly a hundred colonies and protectorates from the seventeenth to the twentieth centuries, from Aden to Zululand.

45   The ratification of a treaty between England and Spain, 1603. (E 30/1705)

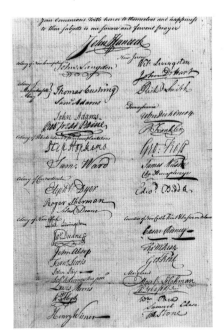

46   The signatures on the Olive Branch Petition, the final attempt of the American moderate party to prevent the War of Independence, 1775. (CO 5/76/258)

47 A page of the log book of *HMS Victory* listing those killed in the Battle of Trafalgar, 1805. (ADM 52/3711)

48 *The Battle of Trafalgar*, painted by JMW Turner. (reproduced by courtesy of the Trustees of the National Maritime Museum)

49 Letter from Abraham Lincoln to Queen Victoria congratulating her on the marriage of the Prince of Wales, 1863. (FO 95/722f. 140)

50 A Second World War propaganda poster put out by the Ministry of Information. (INF 13/140)

51 Letter from General Montgomery to General Alexander reporting progress in the North African campaign, 1943. (WO 214/18)

Eighth Army
1·3·43

My dear Alex

All goes well here. If Rommel attacks me he should get a real bloody nose; I am lining up N.Z. DIV, and by morning of 4 March will also have 8 Armd Bde up and positioned for battle with 100 % tank strength.

That will give me over 300 tanks.

The opportunity may well occur to dot him one, then catch him on the rebound and follow him up.

Anyhow I shall not let anything stop PUGILIST on 20 March.

If Rommel develops an attack against me I should want you to bomb his rear concentrations; while I will deal with his forward troops.

Yrs ever
Monty

Month and Year JANUARY 1951.   W A R   D I A R Y   Unit:- 27 BRITISH COMMONWEALTH BRIGADE.

Commanding Officer:- BRIGADIER B.A. COAD CBE DSO.

Place	Date	Summary of Events and Information	Reference to Appendices
NAEGON-NI	18 January	The 5 RCT patrol at ICHON reported observing 200 enemy North of ICHON also 20 men in the town. However, they are not in wireless communication and the message was dropped by air and still has to be confirmed. 3 RAR sent out a Company patrol, supported by 4.2 in Mortars at 1400hrs to patrol ICHON for the next 24 hours. At 2040hrs they reported that ICHON was quite clear of enemy. Lt General Sir Robert MANSERGH KBE CB MC, Commander British Forces HONG KONG, accompanied by Lt Colonel KC SYMONDS DSO, arrived today on a visit to the Brigade. After seeing all officers at Brigade HQ, he visited battalions during the afternoon, and had tea with 1 MX. In the evening, the COs of 2 Chemical Mortar Bn, Lt Col BELL, and 1 Arty Obs Bn, Lt Col O'CONNOR, were introduced to General MANSERGH at Brigade HQ. General MANSERGH's visit gave special pleasure to the Brigade, as it served under his overall command in HONG KONG. He is spending the night at Brigade HQ and proceeds to 29 Brigade tomorrow.	
NAEGON-NI	19 January	Lt General Sir Robert MANSERGH visited 60th Indian Field Ambulance in the morning before departing. The patrol from 3 RAR returned from ICHON and had nothing to report. The Brigade Commander left the Brigade today on leave to HONG KONG and Lt Col A.M. MAN DSO OBE, took over command.	
NAEGON-NI	20 January	A 5 RCT patrol made contact with 50 enemy North West of ICHON. The enemy were reinforced when the patrol attacked their positions. Otherwise there was nothing to report during the day. A Coy of 3 RAR left to patrol ICHON in the afternoon.	
NAEGON-NI	21 January	The coy patrol from 3 RAR was attacked during the night in the ICHON area and later withdrew. The coy was disposed with two platoons on the road North West of ICHON and one platoon North East of the town. A small recce patrol consisting of 1 officer and 4 OR went forward at 1815hrs to recce the foothills across the plain. At 0110hrs, a section outpost North West of ICHON was attacked by two enemy sections. The section withdrew onto the platoon position which was shortly attacked by an enemy platoon, supported by light and heavy MG fire and light mortars coming from the high ground on the left flank. The company withdrew through ICHON covered by one platoon and, having established new positions in area CS 6322, were almost immediately attacked by two waves of enemy advancing across the paddy fields from the North West. A battle ensued and the attacks were beaten off. The rearguard patrol rejoined the company without incident and the company then withdrew to its own lines. Enemy casualties were estimated at 10 killed and 15 wounded while 3 RARs casualties were 1 killed, 2 wounded and 1 officer and 4 OR missing from the recce patrol.	Map at Appendix "A"

52   The Korean War diary of the 27th brigade, reporting the visit of Lieutenant-General Sir Horace Robertson to Uijong-Bu in December 1950. (WO 281/709)

53   The photograph shows Major Gwin speaking to Corporals Anderson, Boorman, Porter, Houchen, Pegg and Amos. (reproduced by permission of the Imperial War Museum)

Kings and queens

In the nine hundred year old archive of a kingdom the names of the monarchs inevitably appear many millions of times and there are some letters and papers of a personal nature which date from the time when kings were actively involved in the business of government. Signatures and letters of some of the medieval rulers and their families survive, but it is in the Tudor and Stuart period, when records become more abundant and kings more literate, that there is the greatest chance of finding royal memorabilia.

54 Letters of Edward III conferring on his eldest son, the Black Prince, the title of Prince of Aquitaine, 1362.
(E 30/1105)

55   Portraits of Mary and Jane.
(reproduced by permission of the
Trustees of the National Portrait
Gallery)

56   Letter from Princess Mary to her
stepmother, Jane Seymour, pleading for
a reconciliation with her father, Henry
VIII, 'My moste mercifull and benyngne
father, who hathe the hoole dispocition
of myn harte in hys noble hande', 1536.
(SP 1/104 f. 223)

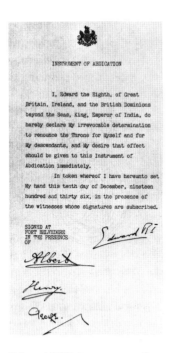

59　Photograph of Her Majesty taken by Cecil Beaton. (Camera Press, London)

60　The oath taken by Her Majesty The Queen at her coronation in 1953. (C 57/17)

57　Edward VIII's instrument of abdication, 1936. (PC 11/1)

58　Photograph of the Duke and Duchess of Windsor taken by Cecil Beaton. (reproduced by permission of the Trustees of the National Portrait Gallery)

I solemnly promise and swear to govern the Peoples of the United Kingdom of Great Britain and Northern Ireland, Canada, Australia, New Zealand and the Union of South Africa, Pakistan and Ceylon, and of my Possessions and the other Territories to any of them belonging or pertaining, according to their respective laws and customs.

I will to my power cause Law and Justice, in Mercy, to be executed in all my judgements.

I will to the utmost of my power maintain the Laws of God and the true profession of the Gospel. I will to the utmost of my power maintain in the United Kingdom the Protestant Reformed Religion established by law. And I will maintain and preserve inviolably the settlement of the Church of England, and the doctrine, worship, discipline, and government thereof, as by law established in England. And I will preserve unto the Bishops and Clergy of England, and to the Churches there committed to their charge, all such rights and privileges as by law do or shall appertain to them or any of them.

The things which I have here before promised, I will perform and keep.

So help me God.

The law

The administration of justice started with the king in his court settling disagreements between his subjects. From early medieval times judges were appointed to help in the Curia Regis and there evolved a system whereby they travelled round the realm, imposing the king's peace and reducing the legal competence of the local courts held by manorial lords and others. Slowly two great courts emerged, King's Bench and Common Pleas, where routine judicial business, both civil and criminal, was conducted. These became known as the courts of common law. Meanwhile the king in council continued to deal with matters of high importance and from this operation developed the equity courts of Chancery, Star Chamber, Requests and the rest, dispensing a more flexible sort of justice with summary proceedings and records which were kept in English not Latin.

The legal records in the Office represent 800 years of litigation and criminal prosecution. The first Curia Regis roll dates from the reign of Richard I and the Plea Rolls, numbering over 4000, run in unbroken series from the time of Edward I to that of Queen Victoria. The most accessible and popular legal source from the late fifteenth century onwards are the voluminous Chancery proceedings, which document in close detail the squabbles of land owners, merchants and shopkeepers over rights, money and property. Information about modern criminal cases can be found among the records of the Metropolitan Police, the Director of Public Prosecutions, the Assizes and the Old Bailey, the Prison Commission and the Home Office.

61   Indictment of Dick Turpin (going by the name of John Palmer) for horse stealing. The notorious highwayman was tried at the York Assizes, found guilty and hanged, 1739. (ASSI 44/54)

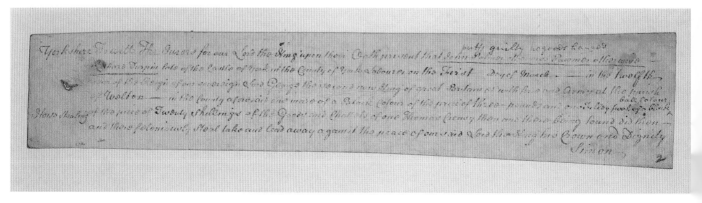

Commercial Street

Metropolitan Police.

H Division.

12th November 1888

At 6 pm 12th George Hutchinson of the Victoria Home Commercial Street came to this Station and made the following statement.

About 2 am 9th I was coming by Thrawl Street Commercial Street. and just before I got to Flower and Dean Street. I met the Murdered woman Kelly. and she said to me Hutchinson will you lend me sixpence. I said I can't I have spent all my money going down to Romford she said good morning I must go and find some money. she went away towards Thrawl Street. a man coming in the opposite direction to Kelly. tapped her on the shoulder and said something to her they both burst out laughing. I heard her say alright to him. and the man said you will be alright. for what I have told you. he then placed his right hand around her shoulders. He also had a kind of a small parcel in his left hand. with a kind of a strap round it. I stood against the lamp of the Queens Head Public House. and watched him. They both then came past me and the man hid down his head. with his hat over his eyes. I stooped down and looked him in the face. He looked at me

George Hutchinson

62   Evidence given to the police by George Hutchinson in the 'Jack the Ripper' case, 1888. (MEPO 3/140)

63   Exhibits produced in the celebrated Tichborne case, conducted in the Chancery Division, 1871. An adventurer called Arthur Orton laid claim to the Tichborne baronetcy and fortune, pretending to be the son of the heir to the title who had drowned at sea. He lost the Chancery case and was subsequently convicted of perjury. The two trials cost £90,000 which was paid out of the estate. (J 90/1223)

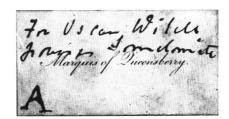

64   The Marquis of Queensberry's visiting card produced as evidence in the trial of Oscar Wilde for homosexual offences, 1895. (CRIM 1/41)

65   Photograph of John Wilkes preserved among the records of the Prison Commission. He was a waterman who was sentenced at Lambeth to twenty one days' hard labour for stealing an anchor, 1873. (PCOM 2/291)

Trade and industry

In the last hundred years government has become increasingly concerned with the regulation of commerce and the running of industry.

66   Advertisement for Jacobs' lager submitted for copyright registration. (COPY 1/84 no. 283)

67 The original art work for the HMV
trade mark, submitted for copyright
registration in 1899. (COPY 1/147)

68 'VC at pit bottom', a photograph
from the National Coal Board's Cobb
Collection showing miners in a pit at
Eastwood in Nottinghamshire, between
1907 and 1914. (COPY 13/110)

Maps

The Public Record Office holds what is probably the largest single archival accumulation of maps and plans in the world, many of which relate to territories formerly belonging to the British Empire. Reproduced below is one of the finest plans of a medieval manor which survives.

69   Plan of Chertsey Abbey and its estates, fifteenth century.
(E 164/25 m 222)

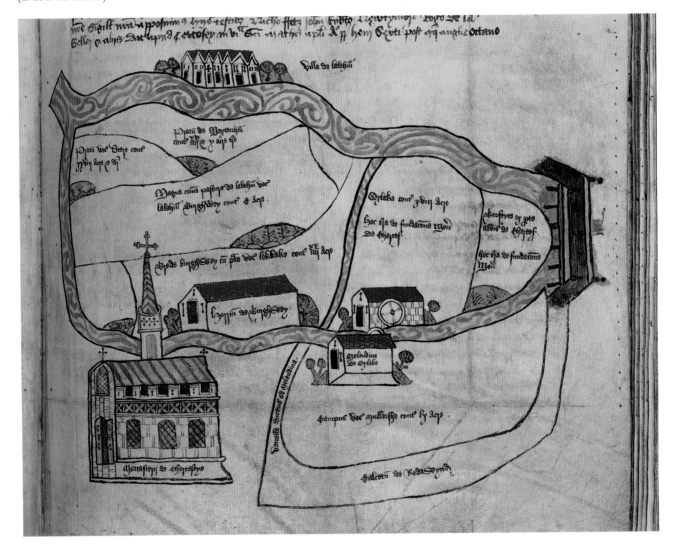

Our ancestors

As government concern with the ordinary subject increased the common man entered the public records. The Domesday survey of 1086 names the chief landowners in a country of about one and a half million people. The 1881 census returns list every single person in the land, 25,794,000 souls. Domesday was written up in two thick registers; the 1881 census enumerators' books number 5,643 and occupy 460 feet of shelving.

The PRO is not the first port of call for the would-be genealogist. Before coming to Chancery Lane, Kew or Portugal Street he should trace his family back through the records of the registration of births, marriages and death held by the Registrar General in St Catherine's House. Registration started in 1837 in England and Wales; before that date the 'vital records' are the entries made by clergymen in their parish registers, noting the baptisms, marriages and burials they had conducted. Most parish registers are held in country records offices and some go back as far as the sixteenth century.

Research in the PRO serves to supplement information found elsewhere, providing extra ancestors, details about careers and possessions, perhaps shedding light on skeletons in the family cupboard. Among the service records there may even be a physical description of an ancestor who served in the army, navy or merchant navy.

The great nineteenth-century censuses provide the most comprehensive material for the growing body of ancestor hunters and for anyone researching the history of a town or village. Censuses were taken every ten years from 1801; from 1841 the enumerators were required to note the names, ages, and other details of the household they were investigating.

The undermentioned Houses are situate within the Boundaries of the

Civil Parish [or Township] of	City or Municipal Borough of	Municipal Ward of	Parliamentary Borough of	Town of	Village or Hamlet, &c., of	Local Board, or [Improvement Commissioners District] of	Ecclesiastical D
Bethnal Green		South	Hackney			Bethnal Green	St Ana

No. of Schedule	ROAD, STREET, &c., and No. or NAME of HOUSE	HOUSES Inhabited	Uninhabited (U.), or Building (B.)	NAME and Surname of each Person	RELATION to Head of Family	CON-DITION	AGE of Males	AGE of Females	Rank, Profession, or OCCUPATION	WHERE BORN	W 1. Deaf 2. Blind 3. Imbe 4. Luna
7	9 Hague Street	1		Thomas Short	Head	Mar	37		Oil Shopman	Middlesex Bethnal Green	
				Sarah Do	Wife	Mar		37	Do	Herefordshire	
				Thomas Do	Son	Unm	16		Oil Shopman	Middlesex Bethnal Green	
				Charles Do	Son	Unm	10		School	Do Do	
				Frank Do	Son	Unm	10		Do	Do Do	
				William Do	Son	Unm	8		Do	Do Do	
				Sarah Do	Daur	Unm		5	Do	Do Do	
				Elizabeth Do	Daur	Unm		3	Do	Do Do	
8				Louisa Lendon	Head	Unm		32	Silk Enterer	Do Mile End	
				David Do	Son	Unm	10		School	Do Bethnal Green	
				Frances Do	Daur	Unm		8	Do	Do Do	
				Walter Do	Son	Unm	1		Do	Do Do	
9				William Talbot	Head	Mar	24		Baker	Cambridge	
				Susan Do	Wife	Mar		22	Tailoress	Middlesex Bethnal Green	
				William Do	Son	Unm	1		Do	Do Do	
10	8 Do	1		Henry Britten	Head	Mar	56		Printer	Do Do	

70   1871 census return for Hague
Street in Bethnal Green, showing the
editor's ancestors, the Shorts, in
occupation at number nine.
(RG 10/495 f.95 p.2)

71   Hague Street, Bethnal Green.
Number nine is marked with an arrow.
(from the Greater London Record
Office Picture Library)

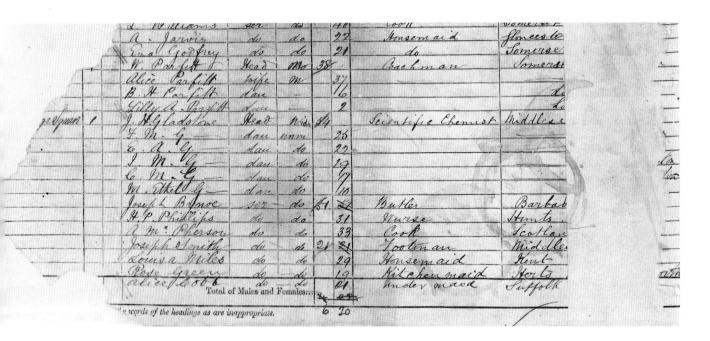

L. Williams	ser	do		40	Cook		Somerset
A. Jarvis	do	do		22	Housemaid		Gloucester
Eva Godfrey	do	do		21	do		Somerset
W. Parfitt	Head	Mar	38		Coachman		Somerset
Alice Parfitt	wife	m		37			do
B. H. Parfitt	dau			16			do
Lilly A. Parfitt	dau			2			
J. H. Gladstone	Head	Widr	54		Scientific Chemist		Middlesex
F. M. G—	dau	unm		25			
E. A. G—	dau	do		22			
I. M. G—	dau	do		19			
C. M. G—	dau	do		17			
M. Ethel G—	dau	do		10			
Joseph Bafnoe	ser	do	51		Butler		Barbados
H. P. Phillips	do	do		31	Nurse		Hunts.
A. McPherson	do	do		33	Cook		Scotland
Joseph Smith	do	do	21		Footman		Middlesex
Louisa Miles	do	do		29	Housemaid		Kent
Rose Green	do	do		19	Kitchen maid		Herts
Alice Cobb	do	do		21	Under maid		Suffolk

Total of Males and Females...

words of the headings as are inappropriate. 6 20

72   1881 census return for 17 Pembridge Square, occupied by John Hall Gladstone and his household. His daughter Margaret married Ramsay MacDonald. (RG 11/28 f.126 p.80)

73   Number 17, (now number 20) Pembridge Square. (from the Greater London Record Office Picture Library)

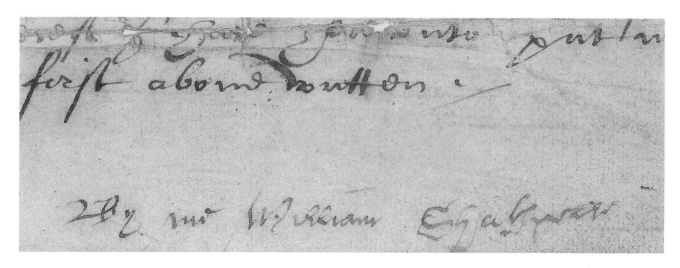

74 The final signature on the will of William Shakespeare. After Domesday, Shakespeare's will is the Office's most prized item. It bears three of the six extant authenticated Shakespeare signatures and there is good reason to believe that those signatures are the only genuine examples of the poet's handwriting which survive. (PROB 1/4)

For many individuals the will is the only personal statement that survives and, as such is invaluable for bringing an ancestor to life. Bequests to members of the family and friends may help to forge links and cast light on a man's activities and interests. The Office holds about 80 tons of probate records, covering a period of five hundred years up to the setting up of the Principal Probate Registry in 1858. It has been estimated that about two per cent of the adult male population left wills before the present century and the Office preserves the dying wishes of many thousands of ordinary people, including the editor's great great grandfather who was a milkman in Bethnal Green.

75 A watercolour commissioned as an exhibit in a dispute over the seventeen wills made by one 'mad Mrs Morice' in the early nineteenth century. The lawyers argued that if she kept coal on her sitting room floor she could hardly have been of 'sound and disposing mind'. (PROB 37/813)

76 Nelson's will. The small leather bound exercise book contains the codicil written just before the battle of Trafalgar. The detail (inset) shows the words: 'I leave Emma Lady Hamilton . . . a Legacy to my King and Country that they will give her an ample provision to maintain her Rank in life'. (PROB 1/22)

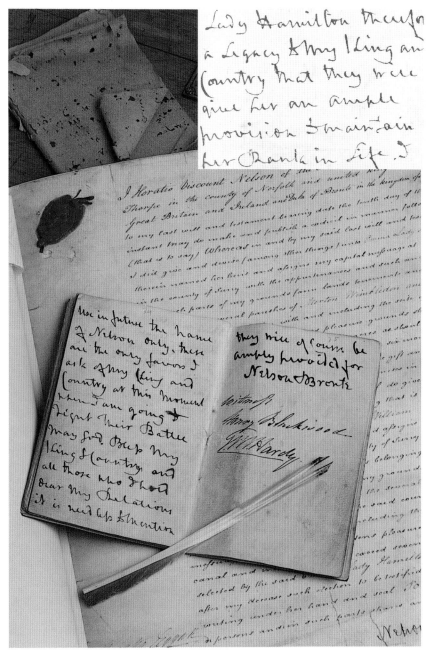

77 *The Death of Nelson*, painted by A W Devis.

78 *Lady Hamilton*, painted by George Romney.

Both paintings reproduced by courtesy of the Trustees of the National Maritime Museum.

Search department leaflets

INFORMATION series

1 Reprographic and Photographic copies in the Public Record Office
2 Admiralty Records as Sources for Biography and Genealogy
3 Operational Records of the Royal Navy, 1660-1914
4 Sources for the History of the Jacobite Risings of 1715 and 1745
5 Records of the Registrar General of Shipping and Seamen
6 Operational Records of the British Army in the First World War
7 Operational Records of the British Army in the Second World War
8 Records of HM Coastguard
9 Division of Record Groups between Kew and Chancery Lane
10 Censuses of Population, 1801-1881
11 Records of the Royal Irish Constabulary
12 Chancel Repairs
13 Air Records as Sources for Biography and Family History
14 Family History in England and Wales: Guidance for Beginners
15 Dockyard Employees: Documents in the Public Record Office
16 Operational Records of the Royal Air Force
17 Handbooks and Catalogues
18 Museum Publications
19 Postcards, Greeting Cards, Notepads
20 Replicas of seals
21 35mm colour transparencies

22 Records of the Foreign Office from 1782
23 Records of the American and West Indian Colonies before 1782
24 English Local History: A Note for Beginners
25 Copyright
26 Assizes Records
27 Hotels
28 Genealogy before the Parish Registers
29 Royal Warrant Holders and Household Servants
30 Chancery Proceedings (Equity Suits)
31 Probate Records
32 British Transport Historical Records
33 The American Revolution
34 American Land Grants
35 How to use the Reading Rooms at Kew
36 Means of reference at Kew
37 Access to Public Records
38 Change of Name
39 Births, Marriages and Deaths
40 Enclosure Awards
41 Tithe Records in the Public Record Office
42 Designs and Trade Marks
43 Operational Records of the Royal Navy in the Second World War
44 Apprenticeship Records
45 Markets and Fairs
46 Militia Muster Rolls
47 Are You in the Right Place? (Chancery Lane use only)

48 Private Conveyances in the Public Record Office
49 Operational Records of the Royal Navy in the First World War
50 Records of the RAF: Research and Development
51 The Ecclesiastical Census of 1851
52 Notes for New Readers at Chancery Lane
53 Metropolitan Police Records of Service
54 Registration of Companies and Businesses
55 How to Read Roman Numerals
56 Tax Records as a Source for Local and Family History
57 The Public Record Office
58 How to use the Census Room
59 British Army Records as Sources for Biography and Genealogy
60 Stationers' Hall Copyright Records
65 Records relating to Shipwrecks
66 Death Duty Registers
73 The Records of the Cabinet Office
75 Domesday Book
76 Records relating to the League of Nations
80 Technical and Further Education
81 Records Relating to SS Titanic
94 Australian Convicts: Sources in the Public Record Office
95 Common Lands
97 Public Rights of Way
99 How to Cite Documents on the Public Record Office

Records elsewhere

LEAFLETS series

6   Immigrants
7   Emigrants
14   Agricultural Statistics: Parish
     Summaries (MAF 68)
28   Royal Marine Records
36   Valuation Office records created
     under the 1910 Finance Act
39   Prisoners of War: Documents in
     the Public Record Office
48   Coal and Coal Mining
50   Records of the Board of Ordnance
51   Captured Enemy Documents:
     Films of the German Foreign
     Ministry Archive
55   Passport Records
60   Statistical Information from the
     Census

The Public Record Office holds the records of the central government and law courts relating to England and Wales from 1086 to the present day.

There are major collections elsewhere: the chief ones are:

The House of Lords Record Office – records of Parliament

The India Office Library – records of the British Government of India

Somerset House – wills proved since 1858

The General Register Office – births, marriages and deaths since 1837

County Record Offices (listed in *Record Repositories*) – parish registers and other records of local government activities

The National Library of Wales

The National Film Archive

The National Sound Archive

Private papers are best consulted through the Historical Manuscripts Commission and National Register of Archives, who also hold an index of all manorial records. There are important collections in the British Library.

Anyone wanting to deposit papers should approach their local record office* or the British Records Association.

Scotland, Northern Ireland (and the Republic) have their own public record offices.

---

* *See Record Repositories in Great Britain*, HMSO, 1987. (0 11 440210 8)

Guides to the Records produced by HMSO

Public Record Office Handbooks

1   Guide to Seals in the Public Record Office (Second Edition). (0 11 440145 4)
11 The Records of the Cabinet Office to 1922. (0 11 440150 0)
14 Records of Interest to Social Scientists 1919 to 1939: Introduction. (0 11 440027 X)
16 Records of Interest to Social Scientists: Unemployed Insurance 1911 to 1939. (0 11 440063 6)
17 The Cabinet Office to 1945. (0 11 440034 2)

18 Records of Interest to Social Scientists 1919 to 1939: Employment and Unemployment. (0 11 440091 1)
19 Tracing your Ancestors in the Public Record Office. (0 11 440180 2)
20 Records of the General Eyre. (0 11 440123 3)
21 The Court of Star Chamber and its records to the Reign of Elizabeth I. (0 11 440191 8)
22 Naval Records for Genealogists. (0 11 440209 4)

READERS AT THE PRO 1963-87/TEN YEAR MOVING AVERAGE

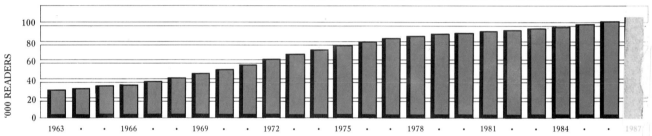

PRODUCTIONS AT THE PRO 1963-87/TEN YEAR MOVING AVERAGE

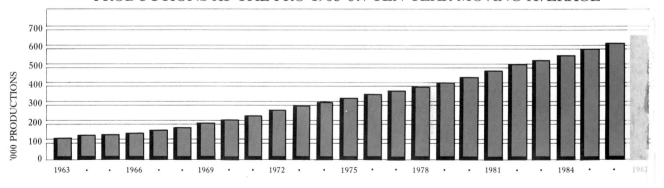

Printed in the United Kingdom for Her Majesty's Stationery Office
Dd 0238646 8.88 C80 561234 12521